J.M. BARRIE'S

PETER PAN

A GRAPHIC NOVEL

BY BLAKE HOENA
& FERNANDO CANO

RAINTREE
A CAPSTONE COMPANY
PUBLISHERS FOR CHILDREN

Raintree is an imprint of Capstone Global Library
Limited, a company incorporated in England and
Wales having its registered office at 7 Pilgrim Street,
London, EC4V 6LB – Registered company number:
6695582

www.raintree.co.uk
myorders@raintree.co.uk

British Library Cataloguing in Publication Data
A full catalogue record for this book is available from the
British Library.

Paperback ISBN: 978-1-4747-0389-5
Ebook ISBN: 978-1-4747-0394-9

19 18 17 16 15
10 9 8 7 6 5 4 3 2 1

Back matter written by Dr Katie Monnin

Designer: Bob Lentz

Printed in China

CONTENTS

ALL ABOUT PETER PAN

Scottish writer J.M. Barrie first introduced his character Peter Pan in the novel *The Little White Bird* in 1902. However, the character's most popular appearance came in late 1904 in the stage play *Peter Pan, or The Boy Who Wouldn't Grow Up*. The play's version of the character turned out to be so popular that J.M Barrie published the novel *Peter and Wendy* in 1911 as a sort of novelized version of the play. Ever since, the character has appeared in films, television programmes, cartoons and even other plays.

Because J.M. Barrie didn't provide many details about Peter Pan's appearance, adaptations of the character have shown him in a wide variety of ways. When played on stage, the role of Peter Pan is usually played by an adult woman!

Peter Pan's costume has changed many times over the years, from a red tunic with green leggings to a green costume made of leaves. The character usually has red hair and blue (or green) eyes. In the Disney cartoon, Peter Pan wears a feathered cap and a green tunic.

In the original play, Peter insists that no one can ever touch him, and the stage directions for the play itself indicate that other characters shouldn't make physical contact with Peter. In one scene, Wendy tries to give Peter a kiss, but Tinker Bell puts a stop to it. It is never explained why Peter shouldn't be touched.

CAPTAIN HOOK

TINKER BELL

PETER PAN

CHAPTER 1

THE SHADOW

All children, except one, grow up…

The family at number 14 was a simple and happy one. That is, until the arrival of Peter Pan

…And then the clock struck twelve.

In this modest house lived Mr and Mrs Darling, and their three children. Wendy was the oldest.

Now that i[s] all for tonig[ht] children. It's [?] Time for be[d]

But you haven't finished the story, Mother.

Then there was John, the middle child.

But you were just getting to the climactic point.

It can wait until tomorrow.

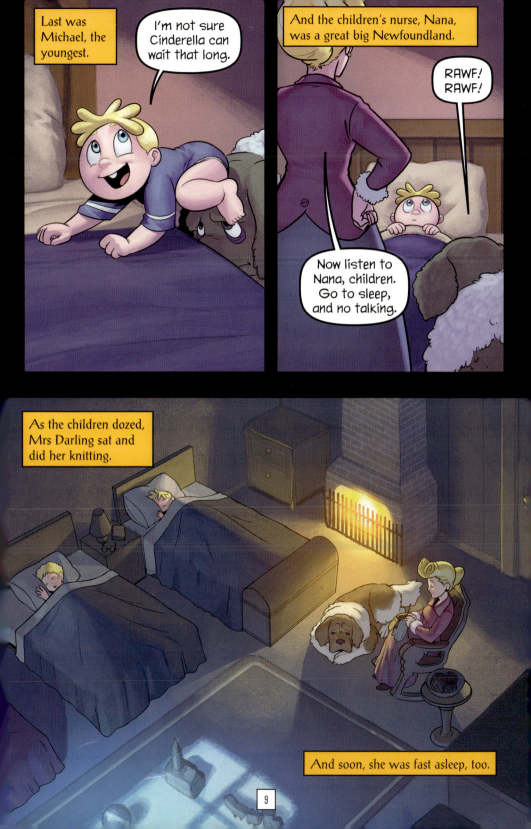

Last was Michael, the youngest.

I'm not sure Cinderella can wait that long.

And the children's nurse, Nana, was a great big Newfoundland.

RAWF! RAWF!

Now listen to Nana, children. Go to sleep, and no talking.

As the children dozed, Mrs Darling sat and did her knitting.

And soon, she was fast asleep, too.

9

RAWF! RAWF! RAWF!

Is it some sort of ghost?

No, it's a shadow – the boy's. It must have come unattached.

Can I keep it?

I had better put it in here for safe keeping, in case that strange boy comes back for it.

Strange boy? What boy?

He flew out...

Hush, Michael.

A boy came in through the window!

I blame this disturbance on you –

You shouldn't be letting boys sneak in through windows at night.

Whoever heard of a dog as a nurse anyway. From now on, we will just tie her up outside...

But, Mother!

Now mind your father, John.

whimper

That's not fair.

One evening, as Mr and Mrs Darling were getting ready to leave for a party, Mr Darling did just as he had promised.

You'll stay out here, safe and sound. Keep an eye on things.

Rawf.

Shortly after the Darlings had left, the children fell fast asleep.

See if you can find it, Tink.

Peter Pan rushed to the bathroom. He found a bar of soap, which he hoped would do the trick.

But when it didn't work...

Boy, why are you crying?

I can't get my shadow to stick.

Don't you know that it must be sewn on?

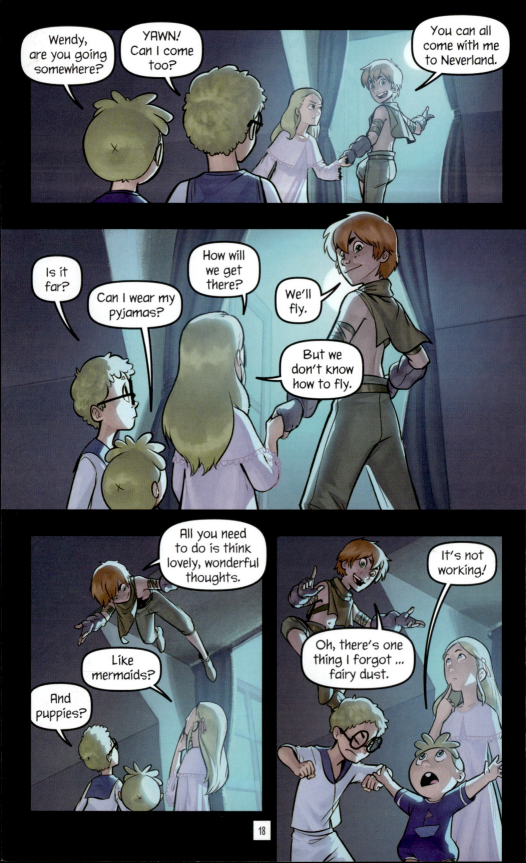

Meanwhile, on the island, everyone had been busy searching for everyone else.

The Lost Boys searched for their leader, Peter Pan

He won't be hiding under a rock.

You never know. Peter is sneaky like that.

TICK TICK TICK TICK TICK TICK

And last came a gigantic crocodile, following them all.

The pirates pursued the Lost Boys.

Avast belay, yo ho, heave to, a-pirating we go!

The Indians were tracking the pirates.

The beasts of the forest stalked the Indians.

As they circled the island, each travelled around at the exact same speed, so that no group caught up with the one in front of it.

But it was one of those boys you hate. I could have shot him dead.

And the sound of your shot would have brought the Indians down upon us.

Then should we go after him?

No, not you Smee. But the rest of you ... split up and look for them.

You and I will look for their leader, Peter Pan.

Was he that cut off my hand!

Then he flung it to a crocodile.

I noticed you have a strange fear of crocodiles, Captain.

Not just any crocodile – the brute that ate my hand! He liked the taste of me so much that he's been following me around hoping to get another bite.

He'd have had me by now, but for lucky chance. It also swallowed a clock, which goes TICK tick inside it. So I know when it's near.

But won't the clock run down one day?

Aye, that is my fear ... wait, why is this seat so hot?

It's a chimney.

And I hear the Lost Boys down there.

TICK TICK TICK TICK TICK

Back to the ship!

TICK TICK TICK TICK TICK

Later, when it was quiet, the Lost Boys crept from their underground home.

Aahhhhhhh!

Oooomph!

Look, it's a great white bird.

It's Tinker Bell, too.

Let's carry her down into our house.

I don't know, and I didn't think we'd find you again.

Where am I? And who are you all?

Hello, Peter.

Where have you two been?

We are your children.

Is Wendy okay?

If you'll be our mother.

But I'm just a girl. I've never been mother before.

That doesn't matter. All you need to do is tell us stories.

Well, I can do that.

Great! Now we should get inside. There are still Indians and beasts out on the prowl.

Not that I'm afraid of any of them.

Wendy, John and Michael stayed with Peter and the Lost Boys for quite some time.

...and when the prince put the glass slipper on Cinderella's foot, it fit perfectly.

They had many adventures together.

Such as the pirate's poisonous cake…

You mustn't eat that!

The pirates placed the cake in one cunning spot after another.

But Wendy was always there to snatch it away before the Lost Boys could eat it.

It'll ruin your dinner.

And then there was the time that several pirates tried to sneak down the hollow trees that the Lost Boys used to get into their underground home…

They got stuck, like corks in a bottle.

Peter Pan protected the Never bird, whose nest fell into Mermaid's Lagoon.

No one is to disturb her nest.

Once, Tinker Bell, with the help of some fairies, tried to carry Wendy off the island.

Wha... is it bath time?

SPOOSH

Another night, Peter challenged the beasts of the forest.

I dare any of you to cross this line.

None of the beasts crossed the line.

But perhaps the most exciting story was the time Peter Pan saved Tiger Lily from Mermaid's Lagoon…

One day, after lunch, everyone lounged around on Marooner's Rock in the middle of Mermaid's Lagoon. The rock had earned its name because evil captains abandoned sailors on it. When the tide rose and submerged the rock, the sailors drowned.

Like Tinker Bell, the mermaids seemed jealous of Wendy.

I don't know why, but they just don't like me.

Oh, of course they do. The mermaids wouldn't try to drown you.

Suddenly, a shadow crept over the rock.

Pirates! Everyone get to shore and hide!

The pirates had caught Tiger Lily, the Indian princess, trying to sneak aboard their ship.

There it is, just ahead: Marooner's Rock, the one Capt'n mentioned.

Sorry about this, but it's Capt'n's orders. No one's allowed to come aboard his ship without permission.

Hook had sentenced the princess to death. So Smee abandoned her on Marooner's Rock.

It can't lift both of us.

Then you must go.

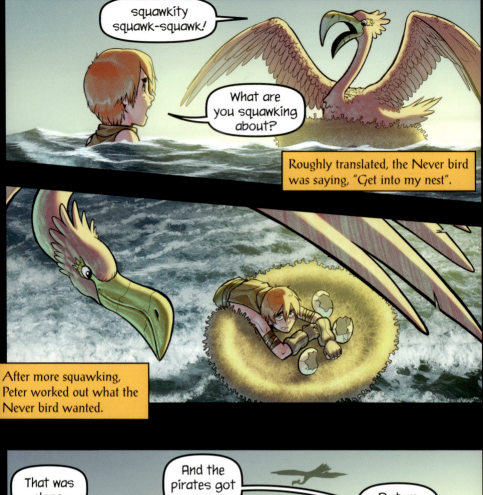

squawkity squawk-squawk!

What are you squawking about?

Roughly translated, the Never bird was saying, "Get into my nest".

After more squawking, Peter worked out what the Never bird wanted.

That was close.

And the pirates got away.

But we did save Tiger Lily!

Peter Pan quickly recovered from his wounds.

The Lost Boys met the Indians near the entrance to their underground home.

Peter Pan, you saved me. We promise not to let the pirates harm you.

We will sit guard as you sleep tonight.

While the Indians stood guard overhead, Wendy told the boys a story.

CHAPTER 4
WENDY'S STORY

There once was a gentleman...

I think I know them.

I think this story is about us!

They were married, and they had three children.

Wendy liked to tell this story so that John and Michael would remember their parents. After all their adventures, sometimes it was hard to remember home.

These children had a faithful nurse called Nana. But one day Mr Darling got angry and chained her up in the garden.

So the children flew away to Neverland, where they met the Lost Boys.

That's us!

I've never been in a story before.

Their mother missed them dreadfully.

Her love was so great that she always left the children's window open, waiting for them to return.

CHAPTER 5
CAPTAIN HOOK

The attack took the Indians by surprise. They were forced to flee.

And that devilish Caption Hook knew exactly what Peter Pan and the Lost Boys would be thinking.

If the Indians win, they will beat on their tom-toms.

TUM·TUM·TU! TUMTU·TUM TUM·TUM

Now wait for them to scurry out of their holes.

An Indian victory!

Let's go and see.

Go without me.

Umph!

Uh-oh...

Come, my dear. I'm sure you'll find my ship most hospitable.

TINKLE TINKLE

Meanwhile, Peter stayed in the underground home, not having heard what happened above him.

It's Hook or me this time...

What happened to your clock, Crocodile? No more ticking? Did it finally run down?

Of course, the crocodile didn't reply. It simply kept swimming towards its delicious prey, Captain Hook.

Bring the prisoners up from the hold!

The two fought magnificently, with Peter Pan's quickness matching Hook's longer blade.

CLANG!

SWOOSH!

Until...

Finish him!

Run him through, Peter!

CLANG!

That would be bad form. He is unarmed. I honour the rules of fair play.

Peter, watch out!

CHAPTER 6

THE RETURN HOME

With Hook gone for good, Wendy and the boys returned home.

As Wendy's story had predicted, the bedroom window at number 14 had stayed open for them.

Let's all slip into bed as if we've never been away.

I thought I heard... Children?

Mother!

Later, before bed, Peter Pan came to see Wendy before flying back to Neverland.

I'll come every spring to visit. And if you like, you can visit me in Neverland for a week each year.

Will I ever see you again?

Each year, for many years, Peter came and took Wendy away for a week at a time.

But eventually he forgot to visit.

As the years rolled on, Wendy got married. She had a daughter called Jane, who loved to hear stories about Peter Pan.

...and I said, "Boy, why are you crying?"

Then one spring night, a familiar figure flew once again into the house.

Peter!

Peter was surprised to find that Wendy had grown up – and that she had a daughter.

Hello, I'm Peter Pan.

This is Jane.

I've been waiting for you.

That spring night, and every year after, Jane flew away with Peter. She pretended to be his mother, just as Wendy had before her.

Then when Jane had a daughter, Margaret, she too took her turn at being Peter's mother in Neverland.

ABOUT THE AUTHOR AND ILLUSTRATOR OF THIS RETELLING

Blake Hoena grew up in Wisconsin, USA, where he wrote stories about robots conquering the Moon and trolls lumbering around the woods behind his parents house. He now lives in Minnesota, USA, with his wife, two children, a dog and a couple of cats. Blake continues to make up stories about things such as space aliens and superheroes, and he has written more than 70 chapter books and graphic novels for children.

Fernando Cano is an emerging illustrator born in Mexico City, Mexico. He currently resides in Monterrey, Mexico. He has been an illustrator for Marvel, DC Comics, Stone Arch Books and role-playing games from Paizo Publishing. In his spare time, he enjoys spending time with friends, singing, rowing and drawing.

GLOSSARY

crept moved slowly with the body close to the ground

cunning cleverness or skill, especially at tricking people to get what you want

flickering quick and unsteady moving of light, like turning a light switch off and on rapidly

jealous feeling or showing an unhappy or angry desire to have what someone else has

lagoon an area of sea water that is separated from the ocean by a reef or sandbar

modest not very large in size or amount

nurse an old-fashioned term for a woman who is paid to take care of a young child in the child's home

pursued followed and tried to catch or capture

ruin damage or spoil

stalked followed stealthily and sneakily

READING QUESTIONS

1. Why does Peter Pan return to the Darling children's bedroom as they are trying to fall asleep?

2. Who is Captain Hook, and why is he so important to the story? What is his relationship with Peter?

3. Why do Peter and the Lost Boys want to remain children forever? Would you want to remain a child forever? Why or why not?

WRITING PROMPTS

1. Imagine that you were one of the Darling children and you had your journal in one your pyjama pocket on your adventures. What would you include in your journal about Neverland? Write about it!

2. Pretend you are Captain Hook. Write a letter to a future reader of this story explaining his point of view concerning Peter Pan and the Lost Boys.

3. First describe your favourite setting in the story (feel free to look back into the story for good ideas). Once you've done that, write an essay that explains why this is your favourite setting.

READ THEM ALL!

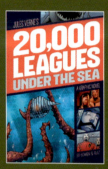

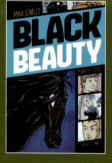

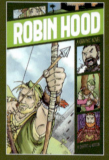

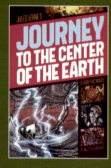

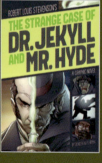

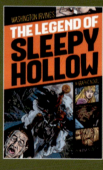

JOHANN DAVID WYSS'S
THE SWISS FAMILY
ROBINSON
A GRAPHIC NOVEL

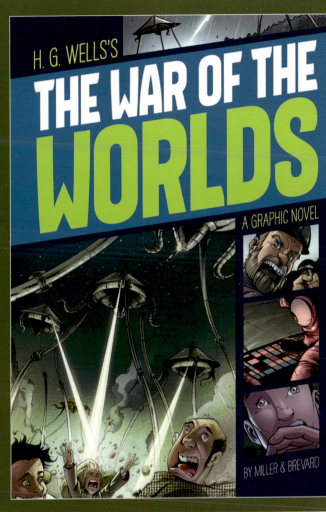

H. G. WELLS'S
THE WAR OF THE
WORLDS
A GRAPHIC NOVEL

BY MILLER & BREVARD

PERSEUS AND
MEDUSA

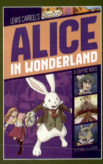

LEWIS CARROLL'S
ALICE
IN WONDERLAND
A GRAPHIC NOVEL

H.G. WELLS'S
THE TIME
MACHINE
A GRAPHIC NOVEL

BY DAVIS & RUIZ

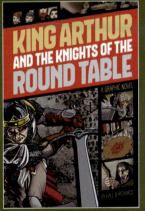

KING ARTHUR
AND THE KNIGHTS OF THE
ROUND TABLE
A GRAPHIC NOVEL

BY HALL & ROVARIS

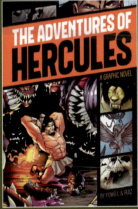

THE ADVENTURES OF
HERCULES
A GRAPHIC NOVEL

BY POWELL & RUIZ